PORTRAIT

—— *of* ——

A WOMAN
USED BY GOD

Lessons from the Life of Mary of Nazareth

Nancy DeMoss
Wolgemuth

*Gracias por tu servicio
hacia el Señor — que
sigas en los camino de El
mientras el te usa para
su reino.*

12/2018

©2016 by Nancy DeMoss Wolgemuth
First printing, 2001

Published by *Revive Our Hearts*
P.O. Box 2000 • Niles, MI 49120

ISBN: 978-0-940110-20-5

Printed in the United States of America.

This booklet is excerpted from the chapter "Portrait of a Woman Used by God" in the book *Becoming God's True Woman*, Nancy Leigh DeMoss, editor. Copyright © 2002, 2008 by Crossway Books, 1300 Crescent Street, Wheaton, IL 60187

What does a "godly woman" look like? How can our lives fulfill the eternal purpose for which God created us? How can we bear "much fruit" (John 15:5) for His glory? Thankfully, the Word of God gives us the instruction we need; it also provides a number of role models—women who illustrate what it means to walk with God and to be used by Him.

Though these women lived in settings quite different than our own, they faced many of the same challenges we face: They were daughters and wives and mothers; they experienced youth, adulthood, and old age; they had to wrestle with the mysteries of life and death, faith and doubt, joy and sorrow. As we study their portraits, we are instructed in the ways of God and find a pattern for our own lives.

One of my favorite biblical role models is Mary of Nazareth. In her life I have found a wealth of wisdom for my own walk with God. Her story illustrates many of the characteristics of the kind of woman God uses to fulfill His redemptive purposes in our world.

The Gospel of Luke records that dramatic moment in which Mary first became aware that God had an extraordinary purpose for her life. As the account unfolds, we are given a glimpse into the heart and character of this remarkable woman of God.

In the sixth month, the angel Gabriel was sent from God to a city of Galilee named Nazareth, to a virgin betrothed to a man whose name was Joseph, of the house of David. And the virgin's name was Mary. And he came to her and said, "Greetings, O favored one, the Lord is with you!"

But she was greatly troubled at the saying, and tried to discern what sort of greeting this might be. And the angel said to her, "Do not be afraid, Mary, for you have found favor with God. And behold, you will conceive in your womb and bear a son, and you shall call his name Jesus. He will be great and will be called the Son of the Most High. And the Lord God will give to him the throne of his father David, and he will reign over the house of Jacob forever, and of his kingdom there will be no end."

And Mary said to the angel, "How will this be, since I am a virgin?" And the angel answered her, "The Holy Spirit will come upon you, and the power of the Most High will overshadow you; therefore the child to be born will be called holy—the Son of God. And behold, your relative Elizabeth in her old age has also conceived a son, and this is the sixth month with her who was called barren. For nothing will be impossible with God."

And Mary said, "Behold, I am the servant of the Lord; let it be to me according to your word." Luke 1:26-38

An Ordinary Woman

There was nothing particularly unusual about Mary. She was not from a wealthy or illustrious family. When the angel appeared to this young teenage girl, she was engaged to be married and was undoubtedly doing what engaged girls do—dreaming of being married to Joseph, of the home they would live in, of the family they would have. I don't believe she was expecting her life to be used in any extraordinary way.

The significance of Mary's life was not based on any of the things our world values so highly—background, physical beauty, intelligence, education, natural gifts and abilities. It was Mary's relationship to Jesus that gave her life significance. We would not be reading this account today if it were not for the fact that she was related to Jesus. "The Lord is with you," the angel said. That is what made all the difference in this young woman's life. And it is what makes all the difference in our lives.

Don't assume you have to be extraordinary to be used by God. You don't have to have exceptional gifts, talents, abilities, connections. God specializes in using ordinary people whose limitations and weaknesses make them ideal showcases for His greatness and glory:

> *Consider your calling, brothers: not many of you were wise according to worldly standards, not many were powerful, not many were of noble birth. But God chose what is foolish in the world to shame the wise; God chose what is weak in the world to shame the strong; God chose what is low and despised in the world, even things that are not, to bring to nothing things that are, so that no human being might boast in the presence of God.* 1 Cor. 1:26-29

Regardless of how ordinary and "unqualified" we may be, all of us as children of God can walk with Him and be used by Him—not because we are inherently significant, but because of our relationship with Christ. Our true identity is not found in a job, a mate, a child, a position, or a possession. It is our connection to the Lord Jesus Christ that gives our lives value and significance and makes us usable in His Kingdom.

MAKING IT PERSONAL

- *What is it that gives my life significance?*
- *Do I believe that God can use my life to make a difference in the world?*

A Pure Woman

Though she had grown up in a community renowned for moral corruption, she was a virgin. Undoubtedly, many of Mary's peers had not kept themselves pure. But when God was ready to send His Son into the world to bring about His eternal plan of redemption, He chose to place the seed of His Son into the womb of a pure vessel. He selected a woman who had not given in to the lure of the world but had kept herself for the Master's use.

In a world that flaunts perversion and scoffs at purity, women of God must be willing to go against the flow—to walk in purity and to teach their daughters the importance and value of a commitment to personal and moral virtue.

You may be reaping the blessings and benefits of a lifelong commitment to personal purity. On the other hand, you may be living with a deep sense of loss and regret from having made wrong choices. Perhaps you feel God will never be able to use you because you have not kept yourself pure.

The wonder of God's grace is that He can—and He will— restore purity to those who come to Him in contrition and true repentance. He cannot restore the virginity you sacrificed, but by His grace, He can restore true virtue.

MAKING IT PERSONAL

- *Am I a pure woman? In my behavior? In my relationships?*
- *Am I pure in what I watch, read, listen to, and in the way I dress?*
- *Am I pure in my motives? My thoughts? My private habits?*

An Undeserving Woman

God did not choose this young woman because she was
worthy of the honor of being the mother of the Savior. The angel
said to Mary, "Greetings, *O favored one!*" (Luke 1:28, emphasis
added). That phrase could be translated, "you who are graciously
accepted." If any of us is to be accepted by God, it will be because
of grace—not because of anything we have done.

> *Nothing in my hand I bring,*
> *Simply to Thy cross I cling;*
> *Naked, come to Thee for dress;*
> *Helpless, look to Thee for grace.**

It's all because of grace. Over and over again in Scripture, we
see that God chooses people who are undeserving. God didn't look
down from heaven and say, "I see a woman who has something to
offer Me; I think I'll use her."

Mary did not deserve to be used by God; to the contrary, she
marveled at God's grace in choosing her.

The moment we cease to see ourselves as undeserving
instruments, chances are we will cease to be useful in the hand of
God.

MAKING IT PERSONAL

- *Am I conscious that whatever is good or useful about my life is the
  result of His undeserved grace poured out on me?*

*"Rock of Ages" by Augustus M. Toplady, 1776

A Chosen Woman

Mary was chosen by God for a task of eternal significance—to bear the life of the Son of God. There is a sense in which God has chosen all of us for a similar task—to bring forth spiritual life. "You did not choose me," Jesus told His disciples, "but I chose you and appointed you that you should go and bear fruit and that your fruit should abide" (John 15:16).

I believe there is a special sense in which God created us as women to be bearers and nurturers of life. Whether or not He grants us physical children, He wants to use us to carry the life and light of Jesus into the world—to be spiritual reproducers, bringing forth His life in the lives of others.

We may look at certain prominent or unusually gifted people and think they have been uniquely chosen by God. The fact is, if you are a child of God, you have been chosen by God for a task of supreme significance—to be a bearer and nurturer of spiritual life by carrying the life of the Lord Jesus to others.

Once you look at your life that way, you'll never again have a "self-image" problem. Many women today carry scars of rejection from parents, a spouse, or friends who have spurned them. What a joy to discover that though we deserve to be rejected by God, we have been chosen to belong to Him and to be a part of His redemptive plan in the universe.

MAKING IT PERSONAL

- *Am I conscious of having been chosen by God to fulfill a specific purpose in my generation?*

A Spirit-filled Woman

We too must be filled with the Spirit if we are to fulfill the purpose for which God has chosen us. When the angel said to Mary, "You're going to have a child," Mary responded, "How can this be? I've never been intimate with a man!" God had chosen her for a task that was humanly impossible.

The task for which God has chosen you and me is no less impossible. We can share the Gospel of Christ with our lost friends, but we cannot give them repentance and faith. You can provide a climate that is conducive to the spiritual growth of your children, but you can't make them have a heart for God. We are totally dependent on Him to produce any fruit of eternal value.

In response to Mary's expression of weakness and inadequacy, the angel promised her God's strength and adequacy: "The Holy Spirit will come upon you, and the power of the Most High [in the Old Testament El Elyon was God Most High, the Creator of heaven and earth] will overshadow you" (Luke 1:35).

I can't begin to count how many conversations I've had with the Lord that sound a bit like Mary's exchange with the angel. The Lord gives me a task, and I respond, "Lord, how can this be? I can't do this. There are other people far more qualified. I'm not prepared. I'm not ready. I'm so tired. I'm so weak. I don't know what I'm doing." He responds simply, "I know. That's why I've given you the Holy Spirit. The Holy Spirit will enable you, and My power will overshadow you and your weakness."

Don't ever forget that you cannot do what God has called you to do. You cannot parent that child, love that husband, care for that elderly parent, submit to that boss, teach that Sunday school class, or lead that small-group Bible study.

God specializes in the impossible, so that when the victory is won and the task is complete, we cannot take any credit. Others know we didn't do it, and we know we didn't do it. We must always remember that we can only live the Christian life and serve God through the power of His Holy Spirit. As soon as we think we can handle it on our own, we become useless to Him. We have to be willing to get out of the way, let God take over, and let Him overshadow us.

MAKING IT PERSONAL

- *Am I depending on the power of the Holy Spirit to be and to do that for which God has chosen me?*

- *Am I seeking a fresh, daily filling of His Holy Spirit in my life?*

An Available Woman

Equipped with the promises of God, Mary's response was simply, "I am the servant of the Lord; let it be to me according to your word" (Luke 1:38). In other words, "Lord, I'm available. You are my master; I am Your servant. I'm willing to be used however You choose. My body is Yours; my womb is Yours; my life is Yours."

In that act of surrender, Mary offered herself to God as a living sacrifice. She was willing to be used by God for His purposes—willing to endure the loss of reputation that was certain to follow when people realized she was with child, willing to endure the ridicule and even the possible stoning permitted by the Mosaic law, willing to go through nine months of increasing discomfort and sleeplessness, willing to endure the labor pains of giving birth to the Child. Mary was willing to give up her own plans and agenda, so that she might link arms with God in fulfilling His agenda.

That was the heart attitude of a young woman named Betty Stam, who along with her husband, John, went to China as a missionary. In 1934, at the ages of twenty-seven and twenty-eight, they were martyred at the hands of Communists. The following prayer, written nine years earlier, explains why she was willing to make this ultimate sacrifice:

> *Lord, I give up my own purposes and plans, all my own desires and hopes and ambitions . . . and accept Thy will for my life. I give myself, my life, my all, utterly to Thee, to be Thine forever. . . . Work out Thy whole will in my life, at any cost, now and forever.*

This ought to be the heart-cry of every woman of God. "I am Your servant; I'm available. Do You want me to be married? I'll be married. Do You want me to be single? I'll be single. Do You want me to have children? I'll raise children for Your glory. Do You want me to be childless? Then I will be a reproducer of spiritual fruit in the lives of others.

Do You want me to live in a small, overcrowded house? Do You want me to suffer with a physical affliction? Do You want me to homeschool my children? Do You want me to love and serve this husband who is so hard to live with? Do You want me to take that young woman under my wing and mentor her in Your ways? Do You want me to give up my free time to tutor that child from a broken home? Do You want me to take meals to that cranky neighbor who is ill? Lord, whatever you ask, I am Your servant. May it be to me as You have said."

MAKING IT PERSONAL

- *Have I made myself fully available to God for whatever purposes He might want to accomplish in my life?*

- *Am I willing for Him to use me at any price?*

A Believing Woman

Following her encounter with the angel, Mary went to visit her cousin Elizabeth. Elizabeth recognized in the younger woman a response of faith to the word of God: "Blessed is she who believed that there would be a fulfillment of what was spoken to her from the Lord" (Luke 1:45). Mary took God at His word. She exercised faith in His ability to fulfill His promise. It was that faith in God and His Word that activated the power and blessing of God in her life. As a result, God fulfilled His promise, and a Savior was born.

Years ago Dr. Adrian Rogers challenged a large gathering with these words: "We have no right to be believed so long as we can be explained." Most of our lives are so very explainable because we are relying on natural, human efforts and energy; abilities and plans; programs and methods.

What would happen if God's people believed His promises and laid hold on Him in prayer, believing Him for the impossible—for reconciliation of broken marriages, for the salvation of unbelieving friends and relatives, for spiritual transformation of wayward children, for a fresh outpouring of His Spirit in genuine revival? We might see God release from heaven the greatest awakening our world has ever known.

MAKING IT PERSONAL

- *Am I exercising faith in the promises of God?*
- *Am I believing God for that which is impossible apart from His power?*
- *How does my life demonstrate faith in the power of God?*
- *What is there about my life that cannot be explained apart from God?*

A Praising Woman

When God puts challenging circumstances in our lives, we either worship, or we whine. I'm ashamed to say I've done more than my share of whining—even about ministry. "Oh, Lord, I'm tired of traveling. Do I have to go there? This is so hard! Why do I have to deal with that person?"

I am reminded of the children of Israel in the wilderness who murmured incessantly. "If only God had just let us die in the wilderness," they whined. One day God finally said in essence, "You want to die in the wilderness? Okay, you'll die in the wilderness!" (see Num. 14:2, 28-30). Be careful what you say when you murmur—God may take you up on it.

But when Mary's world was turned topsy-turvy, when she was faced with a drastic change in plans, she responded in worship and praise. "My soul magnifies the Lord, and my spirit rejoices in God my Savior" (Luke 1:46-47). So begins her Magnificat—one of the greatest hymns of praise ever lifted up to heaven. She worshiped God for His wonderful acts, for His mercy, and for choosing her to be a part of His great redemptive plan.

MAKING IT PERSONAL

- *Is my life characterized by a spirit of praise?*
- *Do I respond to the circumstances and challenges of each day by expressing gratitude for the greatness and mercy of God?*
- *Do my responses to my daily circumstances give the world a proper view of God?*

A Woman of the Word

Mary's prayer in Luke 1:46-55 includes at least a dozen quotations from the Old Testament Scriptures. In those days women did not have a formal education; Mary was probably illiterate. But she had listened to the reading of the Word and had hidden it in her heart. Her life and her prayers were filled with Scripture.

One of our greatest needs as women is to become women of the Word, so our prayers, responses, and words are saturated with God's way of thinking. The world does not need to hear our opinions. When friends approach us for advice about dealing with their children, their boss, their finances, their fears, their depression, or other issues, they don't need to hear what we think. We should be able to take them to the Word and say, "I don't have the answers you need, but I know Someone who does. Here's what God's Word has to say about this situation."

God didn't intend for pastors to be the only ones who point people to the Word. Each of us should be able to use the Word effectively, not only in our worship and our own walk, but also in ministering to the needs of others. If we're going to be women of the Word, we must make a priority of spending time daily in the Scripture—reading, studying, memorizing, meditating, personalizing, and praying it back to God—letting Him teach us His ways.

MAKING IT PERSONAL

- *Do I love the Word of God?*
- *Do I read it, memorize it, meditate on it, and share it with others?*
- *Do I apply the Word to everyday, real-life situations?*

A Reflective Woman

Following the birth of the Lord Jesus, we are told that "Mary treasured up all these things, pondering them in her heart" (Luke 2:19). Twelve years later, after Mary and Joseph found Jesus talking with the teachers in the temple, once again we find that she "treasured up all these things in her heart" (v. 51). The two different Greek words translated "treasured" both mean "to keep carefully; to preserve, keep safe, keep close." In the midst of the many responsibilities of being a wife and a mother, Mary took time to contemplate what was happening in her life and to meditate on what God had done.

The hurried, hectic, harried pace of our culture can be addictive and intoxicating. Many of us find ourselves giving in to the temptation to fill every waking moment of our lives with noise and activity. We get in the car and turn on the radio; we walk in the house and turn on the television or the computer or pick up the phone. Email, voicemail, cell phones, music, and mass media threaten to fill every bit of available space and to leave us emotionally and spiritually empty and shallow.

If we're going to be instruments of His grace who reflect His light into the darkness around us, we must take time to be quiet— to be still—to ponder and reflect on who God is and what He is doing around and in us.

MAKING IT PERSONAL

- *Do I take time to remember what God has done and to meditate on what He is doing in my life and in my circumstances?*

A Humble Woman

Very little is said of this woman after the birth of Jesus. Apparently she was content to be identified as Jesus' mother. She was satisfied to be in the background, not well-known herself, but making Him known. The angelic messenger had said of her son, "*He* will be great" (Luke 1:32, emphasis added).

Mary did not see herself as worthy of God's favor: "He has looked on the humble estate of his servant" (v. 48). In other words, "Who am I that He should look upon me with favor?" She had the spirit of John the Baptist who said, "He must increase, but I must decrease" (John 3:30). Here was a woman who realized, "It's not about me; it's all about Him."

Women today don't always get a lot of strokes for being wives and moms, for faithfully loving and caring for their husbands and children. There is enormous pressure to "do something worthwhile," to have our own identity. Even apart from the pressure of the culture, our own hearts long for recognition and appreciation for the sacrifices we make. The woman God uses is a humble woman; she follows in the steps of the Lord Jesus who "emptied himself, by taking the form of a servant" (Phil. 2:7).

MAKING IT PERSONAL

- *Am I content to serve God without human recognition or appreciation?*

- *Is it my goal that He might increase and I might decrease?*

- *Would I be willing to do all that I do if no one ever saw, applauded, or thanked me?*

A Trusting Woman

Mary trusted that God was bigger and greater than her circumstances. Her trusting heart is seen in the first chapter of Matthew, after her life-changing encounter with the angel. Joseph, her betrothed husband, had not seen or heard the angel. When Mary explained what had happened, apparently he didn't believe her. But Mary knew how to trust God and was willing to wait for Him to act. She did not push her husband to believe what she knew God had said; rather, she gave God time to speak to her husband and to work in his heart.

Sometimes we as women are sensitive to perceive spiritual truth or insight before the men in our lives do. The natural tendency at that point is to think we have to convince them of the rightness or the importance of the insight we have received.

Mary didn't have that spirit. She didn't try to prove anything. She didn't feel it was her responsibility to convince Joseph. She didn't manipulate or control. She simply waited on the Lord and trusted Him to fulfill His purposes. And in His time God sent an angel to reveal to Joseph what he needed to know.

You may be tired of waiting for God to speak to your husband or your pastor or another spiritual authority. Don't try to take matters into your own hands. Wait on the Lord. Trust Him. He will accomplish His purposes in His time and in His way.

MAKING IT PERSONAL

- *Do I trust God to fulfill His purposes in my life and in the lives of my loved ones?*

- *Is there any area of my life where I am trying to work things out on my own rather than trusting God to do what needs to be done?*

A Submissive Woman

We have already seen Mary's submission to God when she said, "Yes, Lord, I'm Your servant. I'm available." She embraced the will of God though it was completely different from anything she would have planned for her life. Mary also demonstrated her submission to God by her submission to her husband.

After Mary's first encounter with the angel, God gave direction for her and for her family through her husband—and she let him lead. To protect His Son from Herod's wrath, God told Joseph to take his family and flee to Egypt. (After what Mary had seen and experienced, it seems she might have found it difficult to take direction from a mere mortal!) After Herod died, God told Joseph to return to Nazareth. As God revealed His will, Joseph led his family, and his family followed.

It's easy for women who are sensitive to the Lord, involved in Bible studies, growing spiritually, and even teaching the Word to others to feel they are more qualified to lead than their husbands and even their pastors. When we communicate this sense of spiritual superiority, we strip men of the motivation to fulfill their God-given calling to provide leadership for their families and for the family of God. If we as women want to fulfill God's purposes for our lives, we must be willing to relinquish control and let God lead through the men He has placed in positions of authority.

MAKING IT PERSONAL

- *Do I trust God to lead me through the authorities He has placed in my life?*

- *Do I make it easy for my authorities to lead me, or am I resistant and stubborn?*

An Influential Woman

In the Gospel of John we find the account of Jesus at the wedding feast in Cana. When faced with a shortage of wine, Mary pointed the servants to Jesus: "Do whatever He tells you" (2:5). She used her influence to direct others to Jesus and to encourage them to obey and follow Him.

When friends and acquaintances come to us with problems, our role is not to solve their problems, but to point them to Jesus and to encourage them to "do whatever He tells you."

Mary apparently was also influential in leading her own children to follow Jesus. During His earthly ministry, Jesus' half-brothers did not believe in Him (see John 7:5). However, by the time the early church was birthed, they had become believers (Acts 1:14); two of them—Jude and James—penned the New Testament books that bear their names. I believe that Mary was likely one of the key influences in bringing them to faith in Jesus.

MAKING IT PERSONAL

- *Does my life draw attention away from myself and toward Jesus?*
- *How is my life influencing others to love, worship, and obey the Lord?*

A Praying Woman

She understood the need not only for private prayer, but for corporate prayer. After Jesus' ascension into heaven, 120 believers gathered in the upper room for forty days, waiting on God to send the promised Holy Spirit. Mary was among those who were "devoting themselves to prayer" (Acts 1:14).

One of the greatest roles in which God has used women as instruments of revival is in the matter of prayer. In 1949-1951 God used two elderly sisters, Peggy and Christine Smith, in the Lewis Revival in Scotland. Both women were in their eighties. Peggy was blind, and Christine was crippled with arthritis. They couldn't even leave their little cottage to worship in the village church. But they knew how to pray. God used their prayers to plant seeds of longing in the hearts of men who then began to pray for revival. God sent a great spiritual awakening in response to the earnest prayers of these two obscure women.

My own life is, to some measure, the fruit of the prayers of a great-grandmother I never knew. As I read reports of violence and perversion in our culture, as I receive letters from women whose mates and children are far from God, as I look at the backslidden condition of so many of our evangelical churches and homes, I wonder, *Where are the praying women? Where are the wives, mothers, grandmothers, sisters, and daughters who are carrying these burdens on their knees and crying out to God for mercy and divine intervention?*

MAKING IT PERSONAL

- *Am I a woman of prayer?*
- *Do I consistently join with other believers in praying for the revival of the church and the evangelization of the world?*

A Devoted Woman

Mary followed Jesus throughout His earthly ministry, even when others rejected or failed to follow Him. She was one of the few who followed Him all the way to the cross. When others fled for their lives, she remained Jesus' loyal follower, regardless of the personal danger or risk.

As was the case in Jesus' day, many so-called disciples today will follow Jesus as long as it doesn't cost them too much, as long as their family and friends are followers, or as long as they are getting their needs met and following Him is rewarding and exhilarating. They are willing to obey the Word when God's ways seem to "work." But few are willing to follow Him when it means a cross—when the apparent outcome is not as they had hoped, when they have to live with those who resist Him, or when there is no end in sight to the sacrifice and suffering they must endure.

MAKING IT PERSONAL

- *Am I a faithful follower of the Lord Jesus—in the good times and in the bad?*

- *Am I committed to follow Him even when it is costly or when others fail to do so?*

A Loved Woman

Not only did Mary love her Son, she was dearly loved by the Lord Jesus. In the final moments of His life, He made sure His widowed, bereaved mother would be properly and adequately cared for and that her needs would be met. He provided means of grace for her within the context of the family of God. She accepted His love and His provision for her needs.

As I travel and minister all over the country, I find so many Christian women who feel unloved and emotionally needy. When they look to the things and people of this earth to fill their emotional void, they invariably end up empty and disappointed. No one and nothing can fill that God-sized vacuum.

But in the Lord Jesus, we have One who knows and understands us, who loves us fervently, and who cares for us and has provided for our needs. The apostle Paul marveled at the incredible love of Christ:

> *Who shall separate us from the love of Christ? Shall tribulation, or distress, or persecution, or famine, or nakedness, or danger, or sword? . . . No, in all these things we are more than conquerors through him who loved us.*
>
> *For I am sure that neither death nor life, nor angels nor rulers, nor things present nor things to come, nor powers, nor height nor depth, nor anything else in all creation, will be able to separate us from the love of God in Christ Jesus our Lord.* (Rom. 8:35-39)

The question is, will we believe His promise? Will we let Him love us? Will we receive His provision?

MAKING IT PERSONAL

- *Am I letting Jesus love me, care for me, and meet my needs?*
- *Am I receiving the provision He has made to meet my needs?*

A Wounded Woman

Eight days after Jesus was born, Mary and Joseph took the infant to the temple (Luke 2:21-35). Simeon, who had been waiting for the appearance of the Messiah, took the Christ-Child in his arms and blessed Him. Simeon spoke of how the Child would be a sign that would be spoken against—foreshadowing the cross and the suffering He would undergo. Then Simeon looked at Mary and spoke words she would not fully understand until she stood beneath the cross of her Son thirty-three years later. On that day she surely remembered Simeon's words, "A sword will pierce through your own soul also" (v. 35).

There at Calvary I believe that sword pierced Mary's soul in more than one sense. First, as a mother she was losing her Son. Even as He laid down His life, she gave up her Son for the salvation and the redemption of the world.

Mothers, have you laid down your children for the sake of Christ and His kingdom? How sad it is on occasion to see Christian parents stand in the way of their children laying down their lives for the sake of Christ. And what a joy to see parents who gladly release their children to the will of God.

I remember when a dear pastor's wife, a friend of mine, said "good-bye" to one of her daughters, along with her son-in-law and two grandchildren, as they left to be missionaries in Cambodia. Just before their departure, I asked my friend, "Isn't this hard for you?" She replied, "Oh, Nancy, I can't think of anything more wonderful than to have a child who wants to lay down her life for the sake of taking the Gospel to the world. Yes, it's hard. We won't see them much in this world, but there's a whole lot of eternity after this life." My friend, like Mary of Nazareth, was willing to bear the wounds of giving up her child for God's redemptive purposes.

Another wound pierced Mary's heart—this one even more deeply than the first. You see, she understood that her Son was dying not only for the sins of the world, but for her sins. Even before He was born, she had recognized Him as "God *my* Savior" (Luke 1:47, emphasis added). As "good" as she was, she was not good enough to get to heaven on her own. As is true with each of us, she had to place her faith in the crucified Son of God who died in her place. As she stood beneath that cross, perhaps she recalled the words of the prophet Isaiah:

> *He was pierced for [my] transgressions; he was crushed for [my] iniquities . . . and with his wounds [I am] healed. All we like sheep have gone astray; we have turned—every one-—to his own way; and the LORD has laid on him the iniquity of us all.* (Isa. 53:5-6)

Mary was a wounded woman—wounded not only by her suffering, but by her sin. As she gazed upon her crucified Son, she realized He was taking her wounds upon Himself. And as she believed, she was healed—cleansed of her sin. Three days later when she learned He had conquered death and was alive, knowing she had been made whole by His death, she joined the other disciples in taking the Good News of His atonement to a wounded, sinful world, that they too might know His healing salvation. For more than 2,000 years her life has provided a portrait of godliness for women who, like Mary, long to be used of God.

MAKING IT PERSONAL

- *Am I willing to suffer in order that Jesus' redeeming life may be experienced by others?*

- *Have I ever trusted Christ as my Savior, recognizing that the wounds He suffered on the cross were for my sin and salvation?*

Making it Personal

As you review the qualities we see in the life of Mary of Nazareth, take time to ponder the Making It Personal questions again and ask the Holy Spirit to make you the kind of woman He can use to fulfill His redemptive purposes in your world.

AN ORDINARY WOMAN:

- *What is it that gives my life significance?*
- *Do I believe that God can use my life to make a difference in the world?*

A PURE WOMAN:

- *Am I a pure woman? In my behavior? In my relationships?*
- *Am I pure in what I watch, read, listen to, and in the way I dress?*
- *Am I pure in my motives? My thoughts? My private habits?*

AN UNDESERVING WOMAN:

- *Am I conscious that whatever is good or useful about my life is the result of God's undeserved grace poured out on me?*

A CHOSEN WOMAN:

- *Am I conscious of having been chosen by God to fulfill a specific purpose in my generation?*

A SPIRIT-FILLED WOMAN:

- *Am I depending on the power of the Holy Spirit to be and to do that for which God has chosen me?*
- *Am I seeking a fresh, daily filling of His Holy Spirit in my life?*

AN AVAILABLE WOMAN:

- *Have I made myself fully available to God for whatever purposes He might want to accomplish in my life?*
- *Am I willing for Him to use me at any price?*

A BELIEVING WOMAN:

- *Am I exercising faith in the promises of God?*
- *Am I believing God for that which is impossible apart from His power?*
- *How does my life demonstrate faith in the power of God?*
- *What is there about my life that cannot be explained apart from God?*

A PRAISING WOMAN:

- *Is my life characterized by a spirit of praise?*
- *Do I respond to the circumstances and challenges of each day by expressing gratitude for the greatness and mercy of God?*
- *Do my responses to my daily circumstances give the world a proper view of God?*

A WOMAN OF THE WORD:

- *Do I love the Word of God?*
- *Do I read it, memorize it, meditate on it, and share it with others?*
- *Do I apply the Word to everyday, real-life situations?*

A REFLECTIVE WOMAN:

- *Do I take time to remember what God has done and to meditate on what He is doing in my life and in my circumstances?*

A HUMBLE WOMAN:

- *Am I content to serve God without human recognition or appreciation?*
- *Is it my goal that He might increase and I might decrease?*
- *Would I be willing to do all that I do if no one ever saw, applauded, or thanked me?*

A TRUSTING WOMAN:

- *Do I trust God to fulfill His purposes in my life and in the lives of my loved ones?*
- *Is there any area of my life where I am trying to work things out on my own rather than trusting God to do what needs to be done?*

A SUBMISSIVE WOMAN:

- *Do I trust God to lead me through the authorities He has placed in my life?*
- *Do I make it easy for my authorities to lead me, or am I resistant and stubborn?*

AN INFLUENTIAL WOMAN:

- *Does my life draw attention away from myself and toward Jesus?*
- *How is my life influencing others to love, worship, and obey the Lord?*

A PRAYING WOMAN:

- *Am I a woman of prayer?*
- *Do I consistently join with other believers in praying for the revival of the church and the evangelization of the world?*

A DEVOTED WOMAN:

- *Am I a faithful follower of the Lord Jesus—in the good times and in the bad?*
- *Am I committed to follow Him even when it is costly or when others fail to do so?*

A LOVED WOMAN:

- *Am I letting Jesus love me, care for me, and meet my needs?*
- *Am I receiving the provision He has made to meet my needs?*

A WOUNDED WOMAN:

- *Am I willing to suffer in order that Jesus' redeeming life may be experienced by others?*
- *Have I ever trusted Christ as my Savior, recognizing that the wounds He suffered on the cross were for my sin and for my salvation?*

Personal Reflections

_____
_____
_____
_____
_____
_____
_____
_____
_____
_____
_____
_____
_____
_____
_____
_____
_____
_____
_____
_____
_____
_____
_____
_____
_____

Personal Reflections

Revive Our Hearts™

Through its various outreaches and the teaching ministry of Nancy DeMoss Wolgemuth, *Revive Our Hearts* is calling women around the world to freedom, fullness, and fruitfulness in Christ.

Offering sound, biblical teaching and encouragement for women through . . .

📖 *Books & Resources* Nancy's books, True Woman Books, and a wide range of audio/video

🎙 *Broadcasting* Two daily, nationally syndicated broadcasts (*Revive Our Hearts* and *Seeking Him*) reaching over one million listeners a week

📅 *Events & Training* True Woman Conferences and events designed to equip women's ministry leaders and pastors' wives

💻 *Internet* ReviveOurHearts.com, TrueWoman.com, and LiesYoungWomenBelieve.com; daily blogs, and a large, searchable collection of electronic resources for women in every season of life

Believing God for a grassroots movement of authentic revival and biblical womanhood . . .

Encouraging women to:

- Discover and embrace God's design and mission for their lives.
- Reflect the beauty and heart of Jesus Christ to their world.
- Intentionally pass on the baton of truth to the next generation.
- Pray earnestly for an outpouring of God's Spirit in their families, churches, nation, and world.

Visit us at **ReviveOurHearts.com.** We'd love to hear from you!